Democracy is Dead: Nietzsche and Trump: Exceptionalism and the Politics of Obfuscation

Keith Pepperell

ISBN-13: 978-1719134576

ISBN-10: 171913457X

DEDICATION

To my children Jack, Alex, and Lydia for whose charming, decent lives I am hugely indebted.

ACKNOWLEDGMENTS

Plato

Aristotle

Karl Marx

Paul Willis

Nietzsche

Machiavelli

Kant

Proudhon

Callicles

Benjamin Carter Hett

Set and Osiris

Lord Acton

Barbara Falconer Newall

Ms. Huckaby Sanders

Mario Savio

Noam Chomsky

and

Sincerest thanks to

DonkeyHotey – Cover Image

1. A VERY BRIEF INTRODUCTION

It is chilling to find oneself part of an intellectually shackled populace in a modern-day instantiation of Plato's Cave.

What is even more direful is that we are participants in a well-known clarificatory allegory, this is all too real.

René Descartes' Dream Hypothesis might be apt here too. He writes "Whatever I have accepted until now as most true has come to me through my senses. But occasionally I have found that they have deceived me, and it is unwise to trust completely those who have deceived us even once."

It will be recalled Descartes largely mistrusted the information received through the senses. He believed that knowledge is acquired through the application of pure reason.

If we apply pure reason to Trumpian trumpeting I have to imagine that he is indeed a Cartesian evil demon who is using daily his "utmost power and cunning and has employed all his energies in order to deceive me."

If it is right that Plato was a dramatist of the life of reason then Trump is certainly a dramatist of the life of the irrational.

The American people have been turned into a game show audience with the seedy on-air cast of fawners constantly changing and being replaced by equally sycophantic simpletons.

The people as audience? Another allegory? Sadly not entirely- but it might serve to clarify.

The audience (I shall call them groundlings) are presently even more than ever deeply divided and the game show producers and the ever slick and slithery host want to keep it that way – and to that end their publicity department works ruthlessly and relentlessly to foster and promote such division.

Divided and conquered?

Such a hackneyed cliché, but sadly clearly one of some merit.

So there we have it.

We the poor groundlings are presently and

miserably living in a groundhog-day-like-Republic.

Democracy has died, but ironically its suicide was both self-made and self-making.

We are now presided over by a pompous toady – a modern day Set.

But whither a Horus to restore the Republic after Set's unrighteous reign?

Will the complex symbolism of The Myth of Osiris and its conflict between order and disorder play out in a real-world-non-violent resurrection of the Republic?

I dearly hope so.

This very brief essay hopes at least to suggest some conceptual groundwork with which to make some sense of why and how the groundlings and an impotent congress placed such a toady – always prone to placing his personal gain (both financial and political) over the national interest – and in a position of near absolute power.

We might expect to find his pardoning all manner of scoundrels purely because he has discovered he can

Certainly Trump is no Hobbesian Leviathan

(for reasons I shall suggest *post*) even though we uncomfortably find ourselves having submitted to the authority of an absolute, undivided, and seemingly unlimited sovereign power.

Were we living in some modern- day state of nature this might have some degree of merit. But we are not, but Trump might well make it such, together with his blundering ill- equipped crew on this floundering ship of fools.

John Locke's *Second Treatise of Government* for example argues that the state of nature was indeed to be preferred to subjection to the arbitrary power of an absolute sovereign.

It will be recalled Thomas Hobbes rejects this and argues that such a "dissolute condition of masterlesse men, without subjection to Lawes, and a coercive Power to tye their hands from rapine, and revenge" would make impossible all of the basic security upon which comfortable, sociable, civilized life depends. There would be "no place for industry, because the fruit thereof is uncertain; and consequently no culture of the earth; no navigation, nor use of the commodities that may be imported by Sea;

no commodious Building; no Instruments of moving and removing such things as require much force; no Knowledge of the face of the Earth; no account of Time; no Arts; no Letters; and which is worst of all, continuall feare, and danger of violent death; And the life of man, solitary, poore, nasty, brutish, and short."

In the Hobbesian hypothetical contract the groundlings submit to the Leviathan to escape this nasty war-of-all-against-all.

But Hobbes intention is surely to provide justification for <u>entering</u> a political society.

When one is actually <u>in</u> a political society surely no purpose is served by submitting to a Leviathan- like toady.

As J. S. Mill asserted it in *On Liberty* society progresses from lower to higher stages and that this progress culminates in the emergence of a system of representative democracy.

The unanswered question is - have we actually made this progression?

Is our 'democracy' currently representative de facto or merely slavishly de jure?

Locke advised the 'contract' with those that

govern is only legitimate to the extent that it meets the general interest.

When we find failings in the contract Locke argues that we must renegotiate it through elections and legislation.

But it was through election that Americans agreed to be governed by Trump and his fawning toadies. Since we have a largely impotent and self-serving congress no legislation in the Lockean sense will be forthcoming.

If indeed we find ourselves in a situation where Trump uses his limitless prerogative power to the detriment of the ends of the people then the right of rebellion is a justifiable Lockean response.

This of course was proffered as the very same justification for the events of 1775-1783 and all that.

Trump falls foul of Rousseau's popular social contract theory too.

It will be recalled that for Rousseau the legitimacy of the state derives from the will or consent of the populace resulting in direct democracy.

So far so good?

However, even though an individual is an egoist – such that his personal interest overrides the collective interest – he should rightly cease to remain such an egoist when he becomes part of 'the general will' — the persistence of equality and freedom in society.

Trumps manifest egoism does just this – it manifestly overrides the collective interest and largely serves his own interest, that of his seedy chums, and that of his always grasping family.

Proudhon's non-aggressive utopian

anarchism argues the best social contract is not between individuals and the state but rather among rugged individuals refraining from coercing or governing each other and thus maintaining total individual liberty.

If only!

2. TRUMP AND THE ANCIENTS

It is often asserted that A. N. Whitehead's well-known claim "The safest general characterization of the European philosophical tradition is that it consists of a series of footnotes to Plato" is intellectually seductive.

I concur that this claim has considerable merit and Plato's rejection of what he took to be the self-destructive political administration of Athens might be a good place to start yet another shortish footnote.

This brief essay (also paying some homage to Nietzsche and other scholars) will argue that in these United States it is democracy rather than God that is now dead.

Frighteningly too, the current cult of exceptionalism is no longer merely evidenced by the rhetoric of nationalistic hubris but rather has been dangerously elevated to glaring instantiations in international policy.

If there is an international policy of this administration one would be hard put to say just what it is.

It is of course largely exceptioanalist and shifts and drifts from day to day with little in the way of a proffered rational prediction of the consequences of its implementation.

Even a utilitarian of the thoroughgoing Benthamite kind would be at a loss to make any semi-rational empirical prediction as to the gross utility of this present gew-gaw masquerading as American foreign policy

Plato might have much to say too concerning the present-day administrative oligarchy in which so many owners of substantial amounts of property hold public office.

We are now ruled by the few and the wealthy and not the many and the poor. Aristotle fleshes this out in his Politics (1).

Sadly, this class contradiction seems of little concern to the mass of groundlings whose ears have been successfully tickled by the vacuous rhetoric of the few.

Even when lurking conspiracies are alleged in

which the oligarchs have conspired against

democracy the groundlings are neither

intellectually able nor politically empowered

to do anything significant about it.

Additionally, when issues of privilege, wealth,

corruption and collusion arise, the oligarchs

draw up their ranks in the same way that

Marx illustrates so well in his German

Ideology and to this end minions and

hangers-on valiantly labor and engage in the

politics of obscuration and obfuscation.

I feel certain that Trump will actively

attempt to punish those who disagree with

him however irrational his claims are

Within this essentially Kantian dialectic, there emerges an interesting cult of national exceptionalism in the United State's social superstructure.

This in turn has created a justified international paranoia based upon the notion of trust.

This paranoia is very evidently internal as well, and is particularly and regularly instantiated in Trump's more than simply 'odd' behavior.

Trump's obfuscatory politics is ever-anxious to muddy the cess-pit, deflect, confuse, and shift attention away from the far more serious matters of how America is being taken to the cleaners and by whom.

Sadly too, the mass of groundlings do not seem to be troubled by any of this since their natural cultural opposition can only partially penetrate the politics of obfuscation and any rebelling against political norms and values is deflected and re-directed creating a substitute oppositional culture.

This oppositional culture is dangerous. It is

entirely irrational and based largely on skin color, gender, and religious affiliation. It is certainly anti-intellectual and emboldens its members to revel in the midden of consistently disrespecting personhood.

The effect of this is to reproduce the social hierarchies in which these simpletons live and under which their subordination and constraints are largely the result of their own (all be it uneducated) volition.

Chomsky identifies the Trumpian class war well. He notes, "The United States, to an unusual extent, is a business-run society, more so than others. The business classes are very class-conscious—they're constantly fighting a bitter class war to improve their power and diminish opposition. Occasionally this is recognized... The enormous benefits given to the very wealthy, the privileges for the very wealthy here are way beyond those of other comparable societies and are part of the ongoing class war."

Sadly, the present poverty of American education serves to produce a weakened groundswell of opposition even though it serves to perpetuate such class hierarchies.

A meritocratic system with unequal distribution of assets and the slavish slogan of 'choice' has produced and re-produced the very same cultural inequalities that much well-argued and meritorious education theory aims to overcome.

Sadly too, the great mass of the groundlings have endorsed, through the ballot box, a political agenda that has created the illusion that the ideas of this political ruling class reflect communal interests including their own.

Nothing can be further from the truth.

The present material and political forces in American society are sadly also the ruling pseudo-intellectual forces that also regulate the production and distribution of ideas. Not unexpectedly, these are for the most part painfully shoddy.

Some claim a new and largely erroneous set of basic norms of logic, epistemology, jurisprudence and ethics are being systematically instilled into the groundlings and replacing the old. This claim is clearly warranted

In particular, the obfuscatory tu quoque

fallacy tactic has been well-employed.

As that consummate master of political propaganda Joseph Goebbels informed,

"If you tell a lie big enough and keep repeating it, people will eventually come to believe it. The lie can be maintained only for such time as the State can shield the people from the political, economic and/or military consequences of the lie. It thus becomes vitally important for the State to use all of its powers to repress dissent, for the truth is the mortal enemy of the lie, and thus by extension, the truth is the greatest enemy of the State."

And,

"The most brilliant propagandist technique will yield no success unless one fundamental principle is borne in mind constantly – it must confine itself to a few points and repeat them over and over."

And further,

"Intellectual activity is a danger to the building of character."

Sadly too, in our present situation Goebbels may not be quite right.

To the groundlings and the present administration, rather than truth being an enemy of the state, it has been relegated to be of little or even no consequence.

When issues of truth become of public debate the politics of obfuscation deflects any partial penetration and employs the groundling's temporary inclination for dissent as the raw material for its reconstitution and redirection often using the tu quoque fallacy.

What about Obama? What about Clinton? What about the Chinese? And so on.

Again, it is an illusion – a Marxist chimera

that the ideas of the present ruling material and political classes are <u>necessarily</u> in the communal interest.

Certainly Plato's depiction of *Callicles* in his instructive dialogue *Gorgias* provides a chilling harbinger of aspects of both Nietzsche and Trump.

Also like Trump, Callicles locates the origins conventional morality and justice in a conspiracy of the weak: "the people who institute our laws are the weak and the many... they assign praise and blame with themselves and their own advantage in mind."

Like Trump too, Callicles' understanding of democratic society involves unmasking and ameliorating what he takes to be the tyranny of the weak many over exceptional individuals among which Trump shamelessly an entirely erroneously places himself.

Callicles states the many "mold the best and the most powerful among us ... and with charms and incantations we subdue them into slavery, telling them that one is supposed to get no more than his fair share."

This certainly provides something resembling

a link to Nietzsche *Übermensch* which he posits as 'a goal for humanity' and which I shall refer to *post*.

In the *Republic* too Plato's clarificatory metaphor of the ship of state provides a further suggestion that democracy is dead.

It will be recalled that the metaphor reveals that a ship to navigate a safe and successful journey, needs an expert navigator at the helm, a captain who knows the capacities of the vessel, geography, meteorology, water currents, navigational astronomy, supplies management, and other related matters.

A seemingly ignorant and untrained person at the helm of the ship of state, however, would endanger the vessel, cargo, crew, and passengers alike. Trump is certainly such a person.

So how just how did American democratic processes produce a non-expert navigator to take the helm?

Like the groundlings in Plato's Athens, the groundlings in Trump's United States are largely unfamiliar with matters of law and ethics, military strategy, globalism, rights issues, economics, and do not use silverware at all well.

Certainly forty years of my teaching in public education has shown a powerful disinclination to acquire such knowledge even at a basic foundational level.

A general inclination towards moderate hedonism has fuelled a paucity of interest, effort, and intellectual self-discipline.

Thus the door is left wide open for Callicles and his slippery tongued chums to tickle the ears of the groundlings with flattery and grandiose promises beguiling them with the nebulous sophistry of the realm of appearances. Trump has partly adopted this Calliclean ploy.

I'm all right Jack if I have a gun, a pizza, a truck, a good dog, a plump little woman at home, a case of beer, and a "shit happens" hat.

Callicles like Trump "articulates a concept of 'superiority' in terms of traditional virtues like intelligence [*phronêsis*], particularly about the affairs of the city, and courage [*andreia*], which makes men "competent to accomplish whatever they have in mind, without slackening off because of softness of spirit."

These have been sloganized and oft repeated but there is manifestly huge doubt that Trump possesses such intellectual virtue and since few, if any, knows what Trump actually has in mind judging his competence in accomplishing goals is at best problematic.

International affairs seem presently to unravel by accident and by hidden hand rather than by intelligent design.

Suddenly these poor ignorant groundlings have found themselves in a state of denial in recognizing they are at the mercy of conditions and under an administration they cannot control and certainly they do not appear to understand just what is happening to both themselves and their nation.

Democracy is dead simply because the groundlings are manifestly unprepared for it.

James Madison (unusually) got it almost right when he bemoans "A people who mean to be their own governors must arm themselves with the power knowledge gives. A popular government without popular information or the means of acquiring it is but a prologue to a farce or a tragedy, or perhaps both."

Groundlings baulk at any suggestion that they lack knowledge and decry those who level criticism at Trump and his slithery posse of courtiers. The present enjoyment of the small trickled own benefits of this economy enables most groundlings to enjoy a modest modicum of fun but also serves to numb them to be content to remain intellectually unchallenged.

Following Plato, good democratic government requires a sufficient degree of knowledge and understanding together with a competent and participatory citizenry.

The groundlings remain closed-minded and do not trouble themselves to even rationally assess whether the intellectual faculties of newly appointed officeholders can be trusted to make informed and well-reasoned decisions as their pseudo-delegates.

When democracy was in its death-throws, and its distortion and abrogation had made it largely dysfunctional, Trumpists have engaged in successfully indoctrinating the groundlings largely through the mediums of television and the internet.

If indoctrination in its achievement sense is

to make a groundling closed-minded to a disputatious belief in that she takes what is false to be true, what is true to be false, and what is a value claim to be a statement of fact the Trumpists have met with considerable success.

Most groundlings have neither the wit nor the inclination to check what they receive via the Trump media against the facts of the real world.

Rather like the Platonic intellectually manacled troglodytes, groundlings seem little concerned whether what they see and have been told to think corresponds to reality or not. Intellectual demands are just that — demands – and are best avoided.

To the Trump administration, keeping the majority of the groundlings in a state of benightedness– produces just the states of political illiteracy, ignorance, and thus helplessness in which the Trumpist basks.

The reduction of voters to an apathetic and poorly informed mass serves to ensure the groundlings cannot even theoretically manipulate and reincarnate the recently deceased democratic processes effectively and for their own mutual advantage.

Plato's shallow 'democratic man' is no different from the shallow minded Trumpist groundlings.

Plato writes, "He lives from day to day indulging the appetite of the hour, and sometimes he is lapped in drink and strains of the flute; then he becomes a water-drinker, and tries to get thin; then he takes a turn at gymnastics; sometimes idling and neglecting everything."

The present Trumpist ruling elites did not create the manifest ignorance and apathy of the groundlings; this has taken several decades, but has successfully used and manipulated these for their own purposes.

3. TRUMP THE PSEUDO-MACHIAVELLIAN BEAST

It is seductive yet largely erroneous to lump Trump in with those naughty Machiavellian Princes.

Niccolo Machiavelli's Florence with all its swampy corruption and its mire of wickedness was no different in kind than the current Washington cesspit.

Machiavelli was right in that felonious actions

are frequently necessary to establish a Republic but recent administrations in the United States have taken this a step further.

If the American Republic is established (and surely it is high time by now) then is it necessary to resort to felonious actions to shore it up and maintain it?

Machiavelli wrote, "It is truly appropriate that while the act accuses him, the result excuses him, and when the result is good, like that of Romulus, it will always excuse him, because one should reproach a man who is violent in order to ruin things, not one who is so in order to set them a right."

Sadly the present talentless, overtly timid, largely self-serving and emasculated congress has necessitated both Trump and sadly Obama before him to despotically rule by executive order.

This in itself evidences the death of democracy. It has heralded the politics of obfuscation and exceptionalism. The central question that must be asked in justifying the use of some or all of tools in the Machiavellian utility belt is whether the end-in-view is to maintain and shore up the

American Republic or is it entirely something else?

So much has been written about "making America great again' and some wags have whimsically responded "It wasn't all that great in the first place!"

The current cult of making slavish references to the intentions of The Founding Fathers and using claimed constitutional rights to justify all manner of mischief has done little to make American democracy immortal.

The ill-informed groundlings have little understanding of the conceptual differences between say conservatism and progressivism and certainly do not appreciate they are nothing other than conceptual terms whose meaning is nothing beyond their intended use in ordinary discourse.

I have often asked a straightforward conceptual question (meta-question) like 'What do you mean by conservatism?'

If there is a response it frequently includes reference to gun rights, belief in God, abortion, aversion to same gender marriage, fear of immigrants, and once a right to park a tractor outside any liquor store.

The answer as to whether Trump is intent on shoring up the fragile Republic or destroying it requires a psychological assessment.

Trump is greedy, of unsound moral character and has garnered wealth and now political power including most frighteningly the power to "legally" kill people. He believes in torture and using military means to attack the families (foreign) of those who have different political agendas. He is overtly paranoid very much in the way that Joseph Stalin was before him. Trump wholeheartedly embraces Stalin's evil 'cult of personality' and has even used the term 'enemy of the people'. Such blow-hardness is Trump's way of avoiding ideological debate and like Stalin Trump has even threatened to physically annihilate individuals who disagree with what he takes to be the absolute entitlements of his office.

He is noted globally and commonly reviled for his preposterous hubris – a towering, grandiose pride in which he revels and postures very much in the manner of Mussolini who despite his brutality was far smarter than Trump and although shorter had far better hair.

Trump's moral turpitude, arrogance, his dispositional interest and blatantly qualm-less pleasure in the cruel and brutal humiliation of others is not Machiavellian.

Mean-spiritedness is a psychological state commonly resorted to by the intellectually ill-equipped who are convinced they know what they are doing but as a matter of fact don't, and instead end up destroying in their attempts to do what they think best.

There is no doubt Nietzsche would have had a field day with trump!

4. TRUMP, HITLER AND NIETZSCHE

Historian Benjamin Carter Hett's significant work The Death of Democracy: Hitler's Rise to Power and the Downfall of the Weimar Republic chronicles the rise to power of Adolph Hitler in the 1920 and 1930s and directs us towards a number of frightening similarities with Trump's current political praxis.

Whether or not Trump can be taken the least seriously we can find many instantiations in his scholar-less bumbling rhetoric brimming with militant pseudo-nationalism, constant threats of economic

and physical violence against his many

political enemies, constant belittling of the

media, a vehement disdain for the free press,

daily lies and revelations of corruption, and

both intervention and utter contempt for

the rule of law.

All very NSDAP.

Further, Trump takes faithful supporters to

be 'real Americans, good and beautiful people

and heroes one and all' with all others as

very inferior non-patriots.

In this confederacy of dunces, the rough and

ready and ever the pompous egoist Trump

ideally served the purposes of an elite and

largely faceless cadre of businessmen and

fading political figures for whom a largely

incompetent non-politician could do their

bidding while thinking it was entirely <u>his</u>

<u>own</u> political agenda.

The extreme right, also brimming with

hubris, saw Trump as a means of eradicating

what they saw as the rule of their inferiors.

However, once Trump had been elected he

became entirely uncontrollable as some very

soon discovered. Lord Acton's cliché would be

particularly apt here.

Whatever the Republican Party now is its elected officeholders presently fawn, cower and cringe and whatever its foundational pillars were they have crumbled into ruins.

Hitler was of course far more popular than Trump, but like Hitler, Trump has always been anti-intellectual and he also recognizes that from time to time it is necessary to spout anti-business, anti-corporate, and anti-elitist rhetoric.

He has also taken the extraordinary step of seeking to repeal anything remotely

Obamaist to the loud bleating of applause from his racist base.

Since Trump's base is almost entirely made up of ill-educated white working class conservatives with more than a smattering of supremacists in their rank ranks a policy dedicated to overturning the policies and legislation of an upstart of color like Obama suits them well.

It does not matter a fig to boorish Trump to even consider the long-term disasters that wait.

An existentialist series of executive orders

that frequently come unheralded and to the consternation of government departments is the new norm in Trump's governing by decree.

In drawing attention to the Washington swamp and promising to drain it, Trump is slavishly following the Nazi policy of creating an enemy of 'the system' in their case the enfeebled Weimar Republic.

While all manner of creatures have been discovered in the black lagoon of Washington, some have claimed they pale by comparison to Trump himself.

Barbara Falconer Newall has argued rather like Plato that the black lagoon is the collective American psyche. She writes "That not-very-bright brain of Trump's has glommed onto something scary. He has figured out how to disrupt the fragile web of mutual trust that holds societies together. He's also figured out that messing with that trust gets him the one thing he wants more than anything else (including the presidency?) and that is — attention. Lots of it."

Like Hitler too, Trump revels in a politics of

division. There are numerous claims of Trump's racism, ageism, sexism, religious bigotry, and general hostility towards all minority groups.

Further, and sadly this is nothing new to Americans, the rhetoric of national superiority and general resentment as to the policies and achievements of almost all other nations fuels both international policies of exceptionalism and internal obfuscation.

The latter has been greatly enabled by the present cult of dishonesty that also shifts attention away from the real state of the

American economy.

If America is doing so very well why is Medicare, Social Security, and Public Education so grossly underfunded? Why do tens of millions of Americans live well below the poverty line? Why do grocery stores slavishly ask their customers to round up their bills to donate to food banks?

Who better to play the Goebbels' role than stony-faced Huckaby Sanders who informed us "I can definitively say the president is not a liar. It's frankly insulting that the question would be asked." Certainly she is minimally on a par with Goebbels and it is entirely and unnecessarily cruel (as one wag suggested) that Goebbels was marginally better looking.

Mario Savio, a political activist in the 1960s may have got it right when he stated, "There's a time when the operation of the machine becomes so odious, makes you so sick that you can't take part." Sadly, the GOP is willing to "take part" and sold their souls as they genuflected and kissed Trump's ring after the passage of an obscenity called a "tax plan."

Hett sums up the Hitler – Trump similarities well when he writes, "Well, the parallel doesn't and won't hold 100 percent. But there is a deeper structure which is similar. The cultivation of hatred against minorities, against the vulnerable, against immigrants and so on. The deliberate cultivation of flagrant falsehoods. The manipulation of alienation and a sense of aggrievement among a group you then use to oppress others."

Trump consistently refers to the stock exchange and the DOW as a measure of his economic success.

It will soon be recognized that Trump

economic policy is almost entirely corporate-friendly and not the least worker-friendly.

Trump recently tweeted that he and Chinese leader Xi Jinping "are working together to give massive Chinese phone company, ZTE, a way to get back into business, fast. Too many jobs in China lost. Commerce Department has been instructed to get it done!" Further, and almost contemporaneously *Agence France-Presse* news service reported that a "Chinese company has agreed to build a theme park at a major Indonesian development project that is set to include Trump-branded hotels, residences, and a golf course—and that will be funded in part by $500 million in Chinese government loans."

I wonder too what striking school teachers thought of Trump's helping out Chinese workers and had to be amazed at his nominee for Secretary of Education, Betsy DeVos, who was entirely confused at her hearing, had no knowledge of public education.

It was later alleged that DeVos was not just an idiot but a dangerous idiot to boot.

Secretary DeVos has, according to Leo Vidal even begun "a public relations offensive to counter the positive press being received by the teachers' strikes that have occurred in several states and seem to be spreading throughout the country. The strikes have erupted as the nation's educators finally are taking action to protest cuts in education funding that have led to low pay, underfunded schools and intolerable working conditions."

Unlike Hitler, Trump has appointed apparently loyal and almost entirely unqualified secretaries of the most important government departments.

Entirely expendable, they will leave

unchallenged each and every of Trumpian

moves however deeply flawed they are

almost certain to

In the Trumpian world of appearances

(mirroring Plato's view of sophistry in its

original sham or 'other that it appears'

sense) the selection of the cabinet can never

be on entirely rational grounds.

It was into the seedy realm of the fat cat

that Trump delved. It will be recalled from

the similar paranoia of Julius Caesar,

CAESAR

(speaking so that only ANTONY can hear)

"I want the men around me to be fat,

healthy-looking men who sleep at night.

That Cassius over there has a lean and

hungry look. He thinks too much. Men like

him are dangerous."

It will be recalled the cabinet included (at

least at the time of writing — they may all

have been thrown under the bus by now):

*Steven Mnuchin, Secretary of the Treasury:

No experience in setting macroeconomic

policy and many problems with disclosing his interests in a Cayman Islands corporation as well as more than $100 million in personal assets."

*Tom Price, Secretary of Health and Human Services: Trades in health care stocks that are affected by the legislation he writes

*Betsy DeVos, Secretary of Education: Alleged near simpleton who claimed that schools should be able to have guns in them to ward off grizzly bear attacks. She had never even stepped into a public school

*Andrew Puzder, Secretary of Labor: Ardent opponent of minimum wage increases and

laws mandating worker rights.

*Ben Carson, Secretary of Housing and Urban Development: Zero experience in housing policy

*Mick Mulvaney, Director of the Office of Management and Budget: Employed a nanny without paying any payroll taxes for her.

*Wilbur Ross, Secretary of Commerce: Undocumented household staff employer.

*Ryan Zinke, Secretary of the Interior: Caught falsely claimed trips home were for the purpose of scouting training locations (allegedly).

*Scott Pruitt, Administrator of the

Environmental Protection Agency: Fervently opposed to the mission of the EPA. Sued the EPA multiple times over its efforts to enforce environmental laws. Had not looked into the scientific research on the poisoning of the water in Flint, M. Not at all likely to stay around for long.

*Michael Flynn, National Security Adviser: An Islamophobe and dedicated loony conspiracy theorist,

*Rex Tillerson, Secretary of State: No government or any diplomatic experience

*Nikki Haley, United Nations Ambassador:

Haley's foreign policy experience consists of going on a trade mission as governor of South Carolina. Apparently has never seen a map of the world.

On the bright side, it is unlikely these folk will survive in office very long.

As Hamilton Nolan suggests "Donald Trump offers less than bread and circuses. He offers only uninteresting insults, unimaginative lies and unattractive baseball caps. To you, his millions of supporters, he offers something else: his contempt. He figures that you are too f****** dumb to see through him. So far, he is absolutely right."

Finally, on to Trump and Nietzsche.

Exceptionalism is the belief that, even while the current US is administration is seriously flawed its activities are justifiable based upon a belief that there is something morally superior about America and Americans generally.

Some might reasonably claim this is an extreme form of hubris.

Globally, America has – rather like Ancient Athens, sought ethical superiority through a long-term commitment to impose two things. Firstly, democracy, in regions of the world—where there is frequently no democratic traditions and secondly, a form of free-market capitalism.

Athens sought to actively punish those who would not voluntarily submit.

After 476 BC Athens assumed the mantle of an imperial bully — something we find in much American foreign policy

Little matter if these two policies de facto and de jure support forms of pseudo-democratic dictatorship and/or extreme forms of economic exploitation. It will be recalled that Callicles in Gorgias supports the view it is better to act unjustly than to suffer unjustly. Socrates, it will also be recalled, claims it is better to suffer an injustice than to perform one.

Present-day Trumpian exceptionalism is used as a double-edged yet crude weapon seeking to provide personal justification for many of Trump's internal activities and also a far more sinister and aggressive promotion of Trumpism abroad.

Part of the arsenal of a thoroughgoing exceptionalist is Trump's use of dishonesty to make his politics of self-serving ruthless power appear to be grounded in sound ethical principles. Clearly they are not

The concept of truth in Nietzsche is important.

Nietzsche suggested, it will be recalled, that objective truth – the view that most of us have come to endorse in the pre-Trumpian world – doesn't really exist. In Nietzsche he considers a former age when

God was the guarantor of what counted as the objective view of the world.

However, when Nietzsche claims "God is dead he means. that an objective, guaranteed, absolute form of truth is now impossibility.

In short, God's ability to determine what is true no longer exists.

The death of God has been a Godsend (sic) to Trump's campaign with his longtime scorn for truth.

The Ubermensch is Nietzsche's answer the

problem of Nihilism.

Put differently Nietzsche's assumption that God does not exist entails that objective morality and inherent value are not possible since there is no ultimate being that exists to create morality and value in the first place.

Trump has unwittingly assumed the role of Nietzsche's Ubermensch whose extreme egoism sees him acting as his own God, giving himself morality, truth, and value as their sole arbiter.

But it is here that Trump has departed from the original Nietzsche an Ubermensch.

Even if Trump has extricated himself from a slave or master position, he consistently seeks to impose his will upon others. Trump may have banished in himself the herd instincts of his groundling base but he is certainly not a master of self-discipline — a key trait of the true Ubermensch.

However, like Nietzsche's Ubermensch

Trump's egoism or self-value cannot be justified by rational argument and logic but can be cosseted by the endless flattery of his sycophants.

Of these Vice-President Pence appears to be the most repellent of the legion of fawners.

He extolled "The President should be praised for restoring American credibility on the world stage, spurring record-setting optimism, signing more bills, rolling back federal red tape than any president in American history" and "fighting every day for the forgotten men and women of America."

And further,

"I'm deeply humbled as your Vice-President to be able to be here. Because of your leadership and because of the strong support of the leadership of the Congress, you're delivering on that middle class miracle,"

Ever so 'umble, and just like Uriah Heap Pence is notable for his cloying humility, obsequiousness, and insincerity, making frequent references to his own " 'umbleness".

Perhaps Pence should have all Americans take an oath?

Perhaps something like:

"You take an oath to a man whom you know follows the laws of providence, which he obeys independently of the influence of earthly powers, who leads the American people rightly, and who will guide America's fate. Through your oath you bind yourselves to a man who — that is our faith — was sent to us by higher powers. Do not seek Donald Trump with your mind. You will find him through the strength of your hearts!"

Certainly this could be plagiarized from the oath to Hitler and passed on to Pence by the First Lady.

The recent egregious election saw the two candidates wallowing in their narrow world-view each refusing to acknowledge any validity in the other and thus fueling the worst kind of politics of division and obfuscation. It has been well-put "For Nietzsche, each perspective on the world will have certain things it assumes are non-negotiable — "facts" or "truths" if you like. Pointing to them won't have much of an effect in changing the opinion of someone who occupies a different perspective."

In summary, we are all in the shit.

We can expect conspiracy theories, claims about undercover spies, deep state conspiracy, doubts as to the legitimacy of any now pseudo-democratic elections, and the swift eradication of many of our fundamental human rights.

Even the Swiss will start charging us for the holes in their cheese.

This year at the time of writing more schoolchildren have been killed in their schools than members of the American military on active duty. Impotent politicians have done nothing so far to remedy this.

Oliver North is now the NRA President. It may be recalled "After testifying before Congress in the summer of 1987, North was indicted the following year on 16 felony counts, including accepting illegal gratuities, aiding and abetting the obstruction of a congressional inquiry, and destroying documents and evidence. Although he was convicted on three counts, his conviction was overturned on appeal on the basis that jurors had been influenced by the congressional hearings, during which he had been granted immunity for his testimony. During the nationally televised hearings, North admitted that he had shredded documents, lied to Congress, and violated, or at least come exceedingly close to violating, a law prohibiting giving aid to the Nicaraguan resistance.''

Great.

A sociopath once claimed ''I think the sociopath has a natural advantage in acting without shame because we don't react the same way to other people's sense of moral outrage. Not that sociopaths have the monopoly on shamelessness, but I do think it is one of our more potent weapons in getting away with things and getting what we want.''

I wonder who that was.

Truth is dead, sociopathy presently rules,

democracy is dead, shamelessness is rife,

but let us hope Nietzsche was wrong

about God.

POSTSCRIPT

Pence do you realize that in addition to deep

state plans and spies there is also

fluoridating water, why, there are studies

underway to fluoridate salt, flour, fruit

juices, soup, sugar, milk... ice cream. Ice

cream, Pence, children's ice cream. Under

Obama Pence. How does that coincide with

your post-war democratic conspiracy, huh?

It's incredibly obvious, isn't it? A foreign substance is introduced into our precious bodily fluids without the knowledge of the individual. Certainly without any choice. That's the way your hard-core democrat works. ... I... first became aware of it, Pence, during the physical act of love. Yes, uh, a profound sense of fatigue... a feeling of emptiness followed. Luckily I... I was able to interpret these feelings correctly. Loss of essence. I can assure you it has not recurred, Pence. Women uh... women sense my power and they seek the life essence. I, uh... I do not avoid women, Pence. But I... I do now deny them my essence. Particularly at $130,000

a pop."

ABOUT THE AUTHOR

Dr. Keith Pepperell is a little-known satirist and occasional television historian who has appeared on History, Discovery and American Heroes Channels. He was born in the 1940s and he has never voted, is a dedicated Platonist, and truly believes the mass of humanity are too feeble-minded to rule themselves the least bit wisely. He has written one hundred and twenty-six other dull books and was honored to be Chair of The Ohio Medieval Colloquium. He also considers himself feeble-minded and certainly no scholar.